SOUTH CAROLINA

A Picture Book to Remember Her by

CRESCENT BOOKS
NEW YORK

Featuring the photography of Chris Swan
CLB 867
© 1986 Illustrations and text: Colour Library Books Ltd.,
   Guildford, Surrey, England.
Text filmsetting by Acesetters Ltd., Richmond, Surrey, England.
All rights reserved.
1986 edition published by Crescent Books, distributed by Crown Publishers, Inc.
Printed in Spain.
ISBN 0 517 47798 X
h g f e d c b a

There are really two South Carolinas. In the beginning, settlements began in what the natives call "low country," a coastal plain that is protected from the sea by a chain of barrier beaches they call "sea islands." The plain gives way eventually to the hills of the Piedmont, which South Carolinians call "up country." The people who live there are as different from their neighbors on the coast as both are different from North Carolinians.

The sea islands, including Hilton Head, one of the Southeast's great resorts, stretch from Savannah to Myrtle Beach. They alternate between tidal swamps and higher savannahs, whose rich black soil produced spectacular cotton crops for antebellum plantation owners. As the plain marches inland, rice and indigo plantations dot the landscape. In the hills beyond, where America's first cowboys once herded cattle, modern America rears its head in the form of industrial plants, shopping centers and tract housing.

But from the very beginning, the symbol of South Carolina, and in many ways of the entire South, is the City of Charleston. In Colonial times it was the country's most important port south of Philadelphia, but it was a city like no other. As an important port it produced families of great wealth, but unlike other American cities, the wealthy became the aristocracy, reflecting the social patterns of London. They lived the good life, sent their children to Europe to be educated, advanced culture and spread their influence inland.

In 1860, when appeals for secession from the Union were being heard all over the South, the up country farmers didn't agree and Charlestonians were beginning to doubt their influence. But they all came together on April 12, 1861 when the batteries at Charleston opened fire on the Federal Fort Sumter across the harbor.

The act may have united South Carolina, but it started the War Between the States and ended South Carolina's Golden Age. Fortunately, the City of Charleston itself survived the war untouched and today it is a city full of treasures, with some 75 pre-Revolutionary War buildings included in a total of some 850 that were there the day the cannons opened fire to change the course of history.

If they respect the past in South Carolina, they have a healthy regard for the future. It was the first of the Southern states to accept, even become enthusiastic about, racial equality in the 1960s, and in the years since it has become a model for other states, even some Northern states, to follow.

Back in 1650, Sir Walter Raleigh said that South Carolina was "God's earthly paradise," with perpetual spring and summer; "a garden shaded by palm trees." He was wrong about the palm trees, but anybody in South Carolina will forgive him that one mistake.

Dionysus by Edward McCartan, at Brookgreen Gardens, Murrells Inlet.

Beaufort (these pages) is the state's second oldest city and has many fine homes (above, top and facing page top). Right: the Tabernacle Baptist Church and (facing page bottom and overleaf) boats moored at two of Beaufort's many public boat landings. Overleaf insets: Beaufort Yacht Club (left) and (center and right) a swingbridge.

The moon sheds an eerie light on the May River at Bluffton Docks (left) and the sun warms the coast of Hilton Head Island, with its discreet holiday homes at Hudson's Landing (facing page top) and sandy beaches (remaining pictures). Overleaf: Hilton Head has many wharves (insets bottom and top right) for those who may have sailed from places such as Fripp Island (inset top) and Hunting Island (main picture).

Previous pages: Edisto Beach and the Edisto Presbyterian Church. The famous city of Charleston (these pages) is graced by many lovely 18th- and 19th-century buildings, such as Hibernian Hall (left) and Calhoun Mansion (top), both on Meeting St. (above) and those in South Battery (facing page), the city's waterfront area.

Three centuries of fine architecture in Charleston reflect the cultural heritage of this cosmopolitan city. Above: Courthouse Square, (right) James S. Gibbes Memorial Art Gallery, (top) Marion Square and (facing page) shady trees surrounding houses at Battery Park. Overleaf: Charleston's oldest church, St. Michael's Episcopal.

Founded in 1670, Charleston prospered as a major seaport and trading post. Wealth also came from the production of indigo, cotton and rice, which was aided by the sub-tropical climate that has bestowed lush vegetation upon the city's streets (these pages). Overlooking Colonial Lake, the elegant houses on Rutledge Avenue (overleaf pages) testify to the city's genteel culture.

Among Charleston's many historic buildings are the U.S. Custom House of 1853 (above), the "Fireproof Building" of 1822 (right), the first fireproof building in the U.S.A., and (facing page bottom) the "Old Citadel", originally a military academy and now the County Center. Top: a quiet, cobbled street and (facing page top) busy Calhoun St..

On the site of the first English settlement stands
Charles Towne Landing (these pages), which was
built in 1970 to commemorate Charleston's 300th
anniversary. It has 184 beautifully landscaped
acres and many fascinating features, including the
Adventure (right), a replica of a 17th-century
trading ketch, and the Exhibit Pavilion (facing
page top), showing artifacts used by the settlers.

In Murrells Inlet, in the grounds of a former indigo and rice plantation, stand the lovely Brookgreen Gardens (these pages and overleaf), where exotic trees and water-lillied lakes provide settings for some of the greatest figurative sculpture in America. Left: *Phyrne before the Judges*, (top) *Riders of the Dawn* and (facing page bottom) *Diana of the Chase*.

Myrtle Beach (these pages), an exciting year-round resort, offers a variety of attractions, such as the amusements on Ocean Boulevard (this page), which include "Ripley's Believe It or Not" Museum (facing page bottom). Facing page top: dawn fishing at Crescent Beach, near North Myrtle Beach.

Myrtle Beach (this page) is the hub of the Grand Strand, a 55-mile stretch of beautiful public beaches, where ocean bathing is enjoyed right up to November. Top and overleaf: "Pier 14", (above) a "boardwalk" and (right) Ocean Boulevard. Facing page: (top) swamps at Lynches River State Park, south of Florence, and (bottom) the Intra Coastal Waterway near Murrells Inlet.

The natural environment is highly respected in South Carolina and many acres have been left unspoilt. Facing page and above: Lake Murray, west of Columbia, which has over 500 miles of shore, (top) farmlands near Conway, and (right) horses grazing in the countryside near Greenville, and at Caughman Farms (center right), near Columbia.

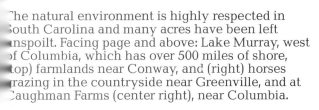

In 1786, Columbia (these pages) was chosen as the
State Capital. It was carefully laid out with
lovely, wide walkways such as the "Horseshoe"
(facing page), of the University of South
Carolina. Top: a statue of Wade Hampton in the
capitol complex, (above) City Hall, (right)
Boylston House and (overleaf) the grand, Italian
Renaissance-style State House.

The Shirt
Shoppe
1212 Main Street

In the upcountry south of Union, on a former cotton plantation, is Rose Hill State Park (these pages), with its grand, Federal-style mansion (top, above and center left). A local event held at Rose Hill is the Union County Bicentennial, shown (facing page) featuring the "Palmetto Light Artillery" Re-enactment Society and (left) the Spartanburg High School Quintet.

Spartanburg (these pages) takes its name from the Spartan Rifles of 1776, a local regiment which won the Battle of Cowpens, in the War of Independence. Established as a courthouse village in 1785, it has grown into a city of some size, with several colleges and churches. Top: Padgett's Creek Baptist Church, (facing page bottom) the Episcopal Church of the Advent, and (facing page top) Frank Evan's High School, with the First Baptist Church (right) in the background. Above: Main St..

Amid the foothills of the Blue Ridge Mountains are several state parks, such as Ceasar's Head (top and facing page top), where one can view the state's most breathtaking scenery. Table Rock State Park derives its name from an Indian legend that told of a huge chieftain who dined at the "Table" mountain (above and left). Further west is the beautiful Lake Keowee (facing page bottom).

Clemson, in the foothills of the Blue Ridge Mountains, is the home of Clemson University (these pages), to which the statesman John C. Calhoun bequeathed most of his estate and his home, Fort Hill (facing page bottom). Other buildings on the campus (top) include Tillman Hall (left), Robert Muldrow Cooper Library (above) and Holtzendorf YMCA Center (facing page top).

These pages: the excitement and color of a football match at Clemson University, with the Clemson Orange Tops versus the Virginia White Tops.

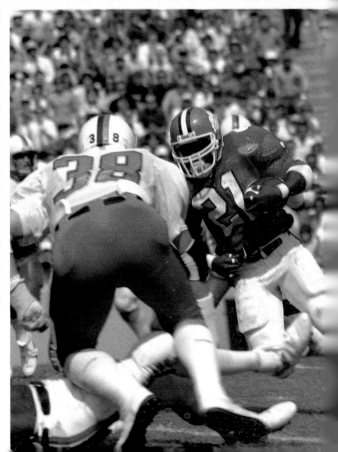

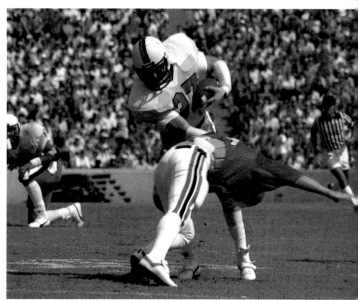

Bright orange clothes mark out the supporters of the Clemson team at a University football match (these pages) where the team's band, the Clemson "Tigers" (facing page top) parade the ground.

Furman University, near Greenville, has many
attractions, such as the Japanese Gardens (above),
the clock tower on the lake (left), James Buchanan
Duke Library (top), the rose garden (facing page
top) and (facing page bottom) Greenville Women's
College, part of Furman. Overleaf: Reedy River
Falls Historic Park, with (inset) Falls Cottage.

Greenville (these pages) exhibits an interesting mixture of architectural styles. Top and facing page bottom: buildings on Main St., (above) the First Presbyterian Church, (center left) the Plaza at City Hall, (left) the Greenville County Museum of Art on Heritage Green and (facing page top) downtown Greenville.

The most exciting part of Greenville's Freedom Week Aloft, which celebrates Independence Day, is the hot air balloon competition (these pages and overleaf), the second largest balloon event in America. The spectacle of a sky full of huge, colored balloons, as well as fireworks, arts, crafts, and live entertainment, makes Freedom Week a very special time in South Carolina.